How to Use Th...

This is a fun book of characters with character!

You will need a Bible and a dictionary to look up the words and verses in each lesson.

1. Look up each verse and choose your favorite. Write the verse in the box.

2. Look up each characteristic in the dictionary and write down two other words that could describe this character.

3. Color the character and think about the bible verses that you studied.

4. Read the drawing prompt at the bottom of the activity page. Draw a comic style picture in the box.

5. Think about each character. Do you want to be like this character?

Use colored pencils or gel pens to color each character.

These Characters are all __POSITIVE__!

| Hope | Wisdom | RESPONSIBILITY |

| COURAGE | COMPASSION | GRACIOUSNESS |

| HONESTY | Forgiveness | Kindness |

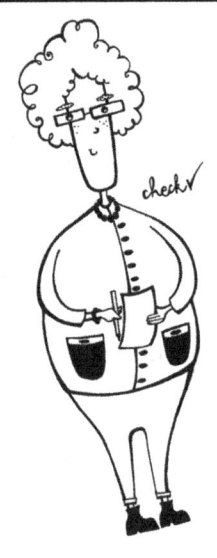

These Characters are all NEGATIVE!

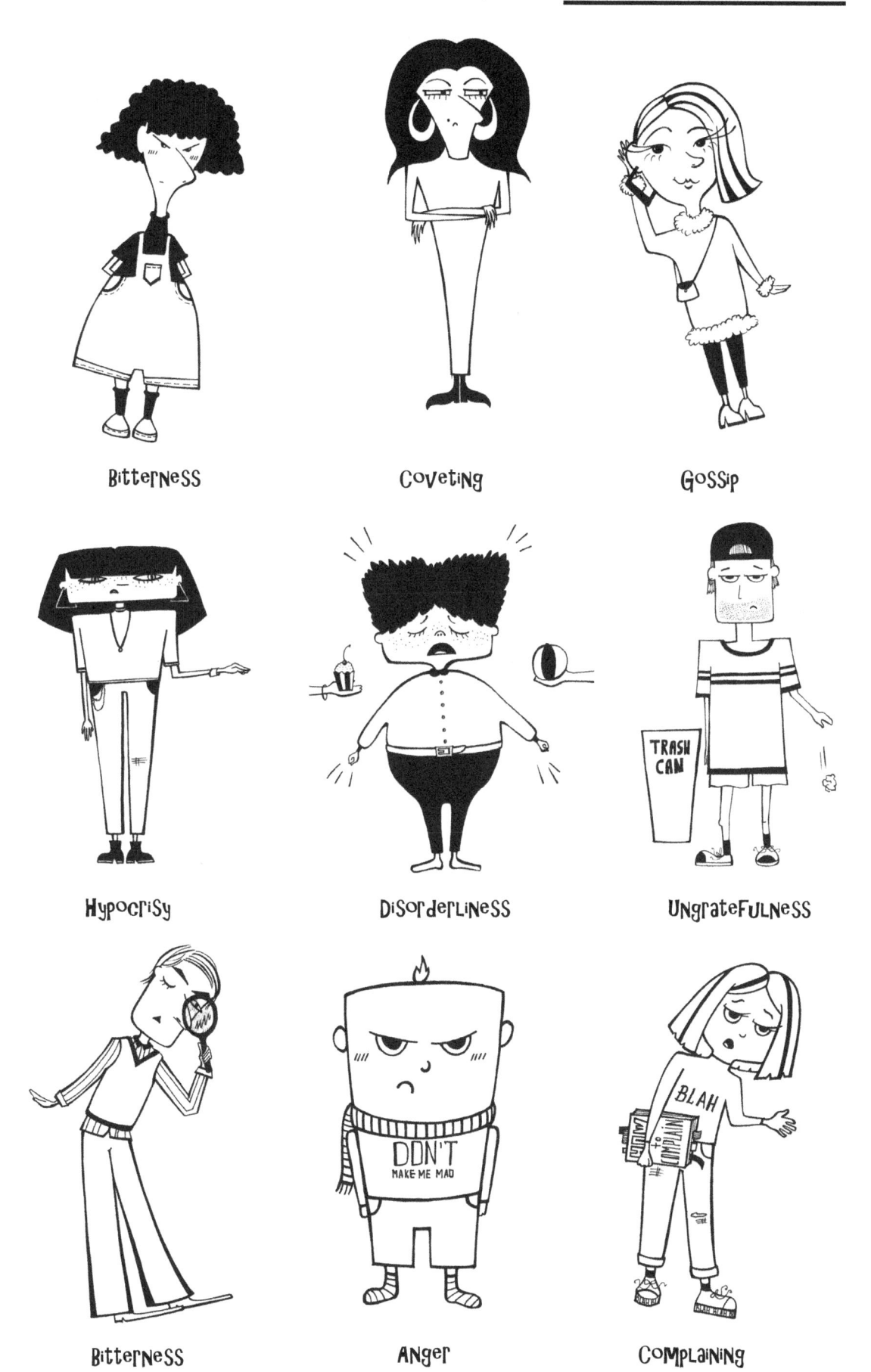

Bitterness	Coveting	Gossip
Hypocrisy	Disorderliness	Ungratefulness
Bitterness	Anger	Complaining

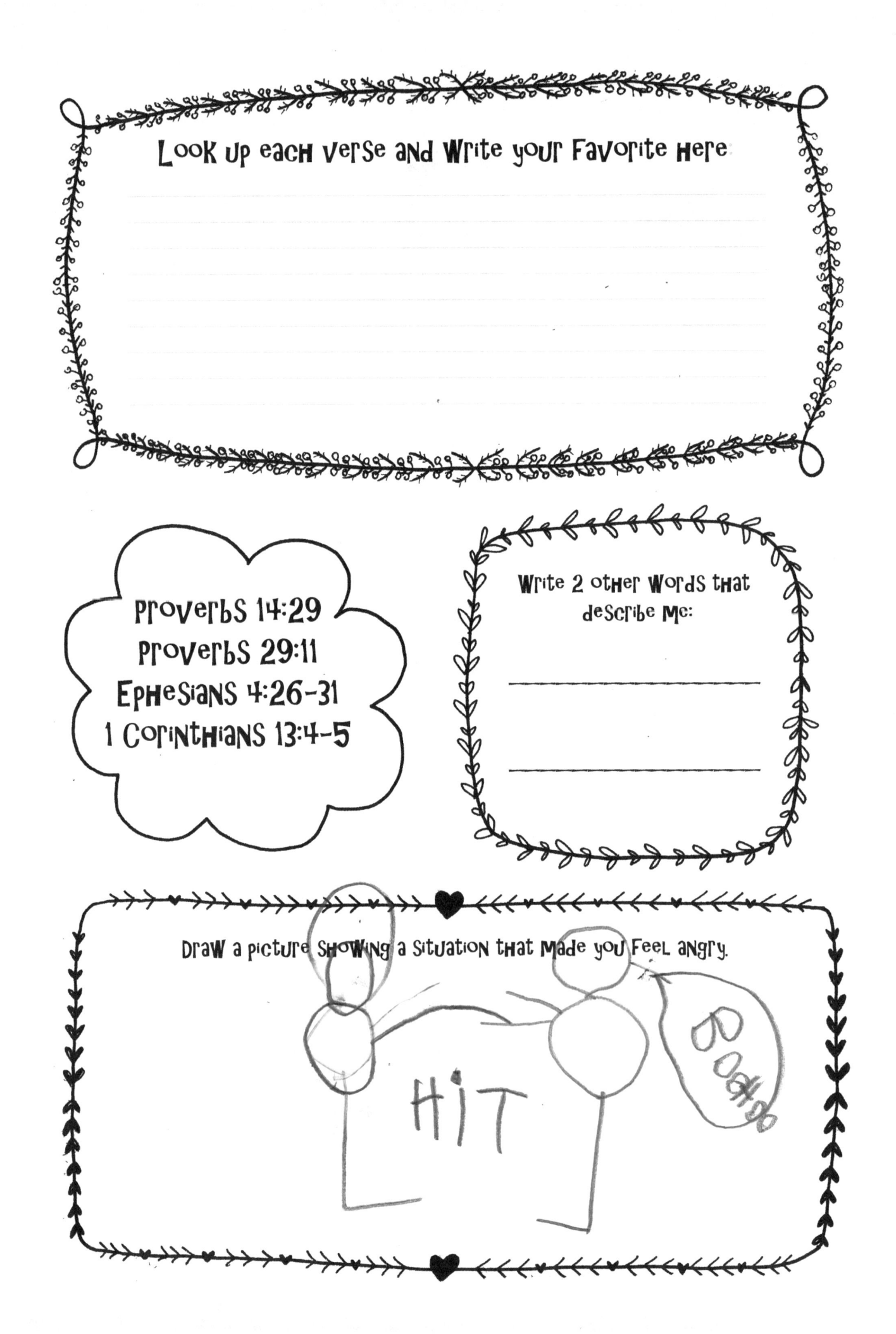

Look up each verse and write your favorite here:

Proverbs 14:29
Proverbs 29:11
Ephesians 4:26-31
1 Corinthians 13:4-5

Write 2 other words that describe me:

_____

_____

Draw a picture showing a situation that made you feel angry.

HIT   Badoo

ANGER

James 1:19-20
Let everyone be quick to hear, slow to speak and slow to anger; for the anger of man does not achieve the righteousness of God.

Look up each verse and write your favorite here

Luke 10:25-37
2 Kings 13:23
Ephesians 4:32

Write 2 other words that describe me:

_____

_____

Draw a picture showing a situation where someone had compassion.

COMPASSION

Colossians **3:12**

Therefore, as **G**od's chosen people, holy and dearly loved, clothe yourselves with compassion, kindness, humility, gentleness and patience.

Look up each verse and write your favorite here

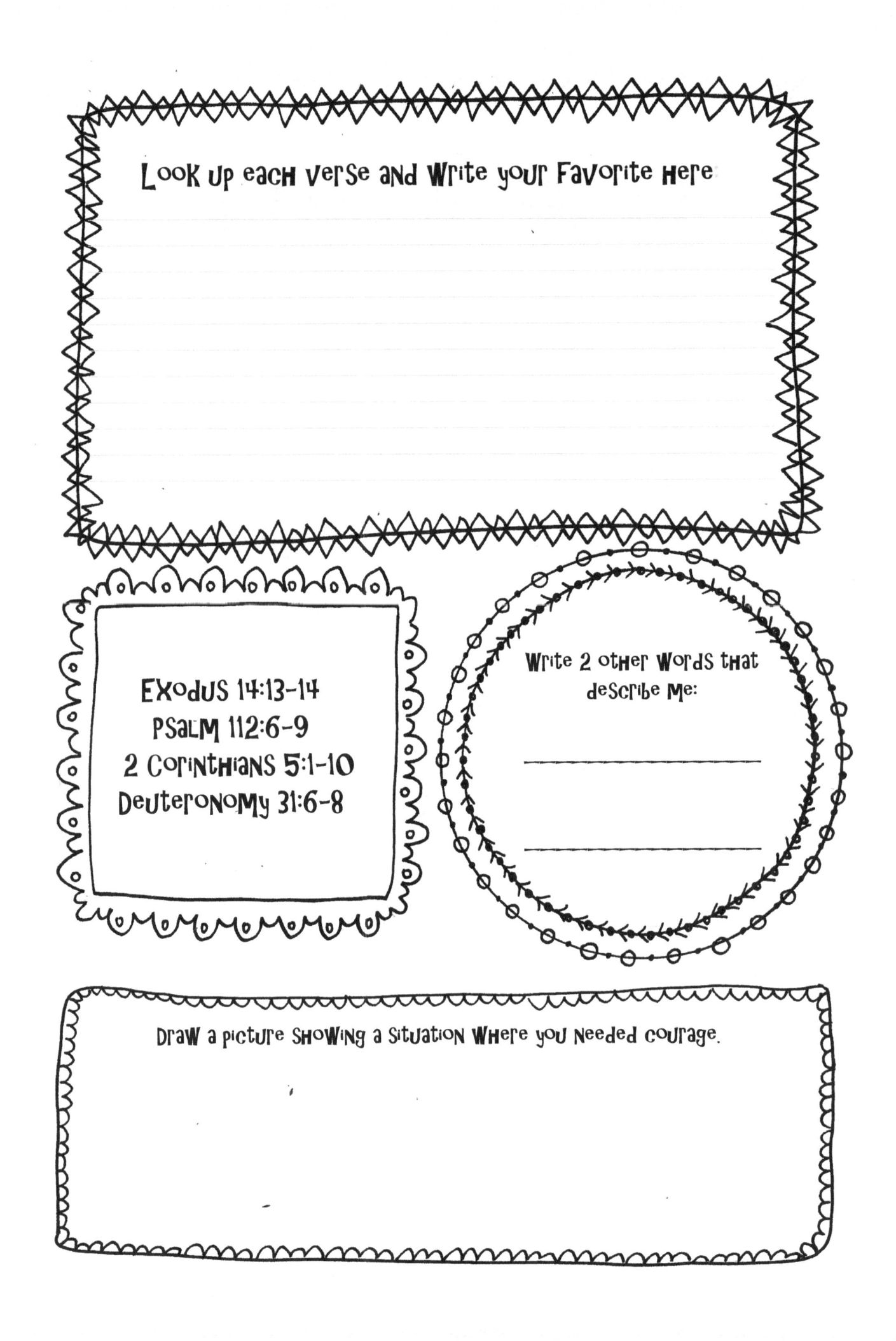

Exodus 14:13-14
Psalm 112:6-9
2 Corinthians 5:1-10
Deuteronomy 31:6-8

Write 2 other words that describe me:
_____
_____

Draw a picture showing a situation where you needed courage.

COURAGE

1 Corinthians 15:8

Therefore, my dear brothers and sisters, stand firm.

Let nothing move you. Always give yourselves fully to the work of the Lord, because you know that your labor in the Lord is not in vain.

Look up each verse and write your favorite here:

Psalm 19:14
1 Corinthians 10:10
Ephesians 4:29
Philippians 4:11-13

Write 2 other words that describe me:

_____

_____

Draw a picture showing a situation where you felt like complaining, but didn't.

COMPLAINING

Philippians 2:14

Do all things without complaining and disputing.

Look up each verse and write your favorite here

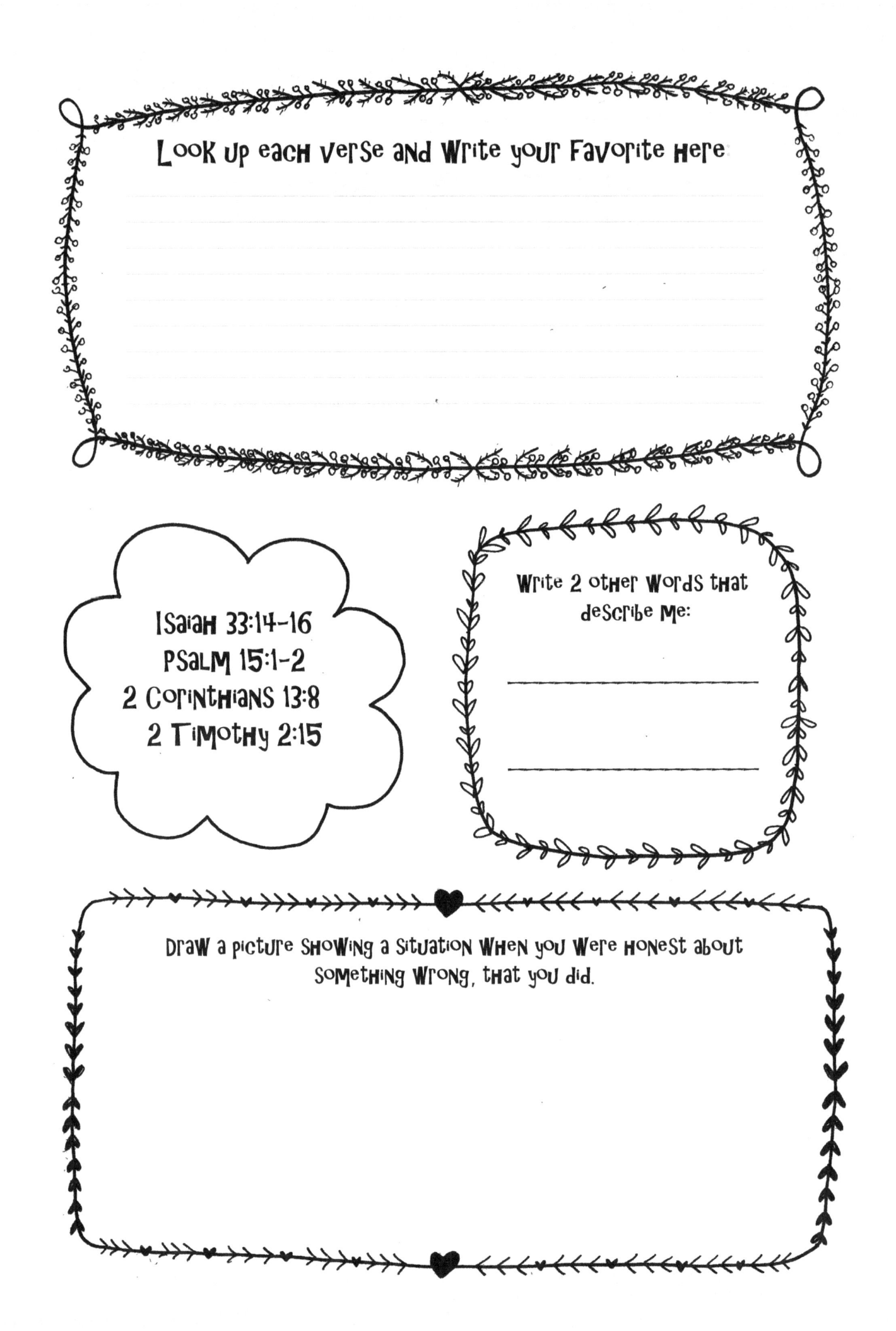

Isaiah 33:14-16
Psalm 15:1-2
2 Corinthians 13:8
2 Timothy 2:15

Write 2 other words that describe me:

_____
_____

Draw a picture showing a situation when you were honest about something wrong, that you did.

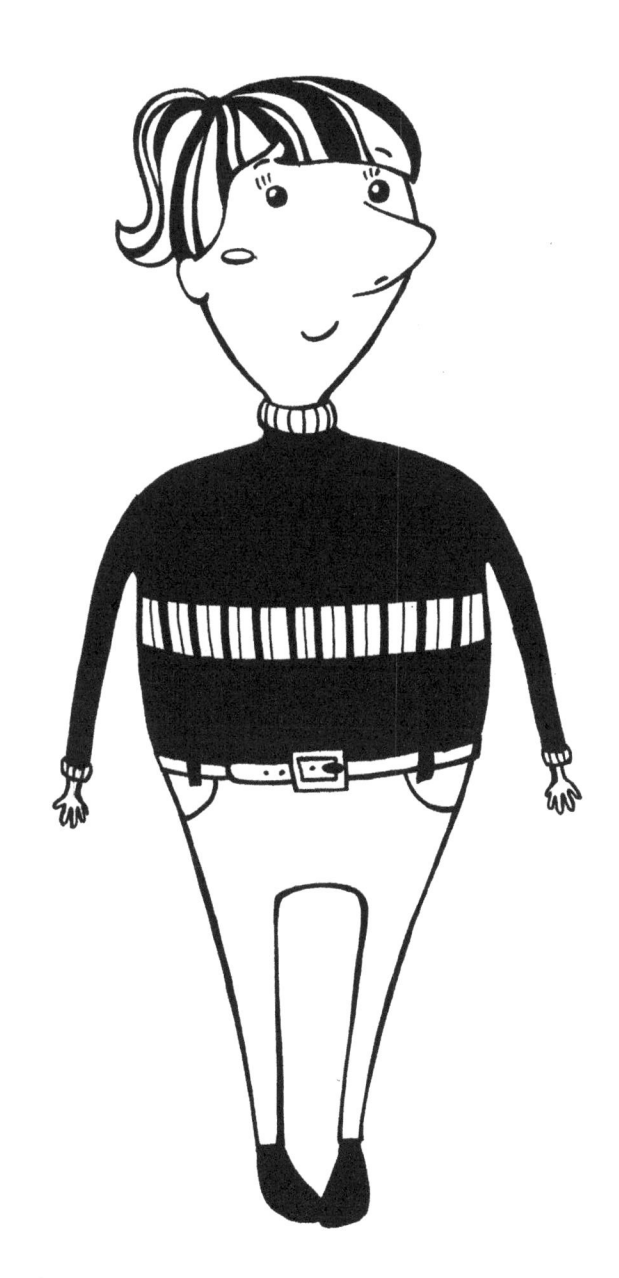

HONESTY

2 Corinthians 8:21

For we are taking pains to do what is right, not only in the eyes of the Lord but also in the eyes of man.

Look up each verse and write your favorite here:

Galatians 5:16-26
Romans 6:12-13
1 Corinthians 9:24-27

Write 2 other words that describe me:

_____

_____

Draw a picture showing a situation where you needed discipline.

DISCIPLINE

Hebrews **12:11**

For the moment all discipline seems painful rather than pleasant, but later it yields the peaceful fruit of righteousness to those who have been trained by it.

Look up each verse and write your favorite here

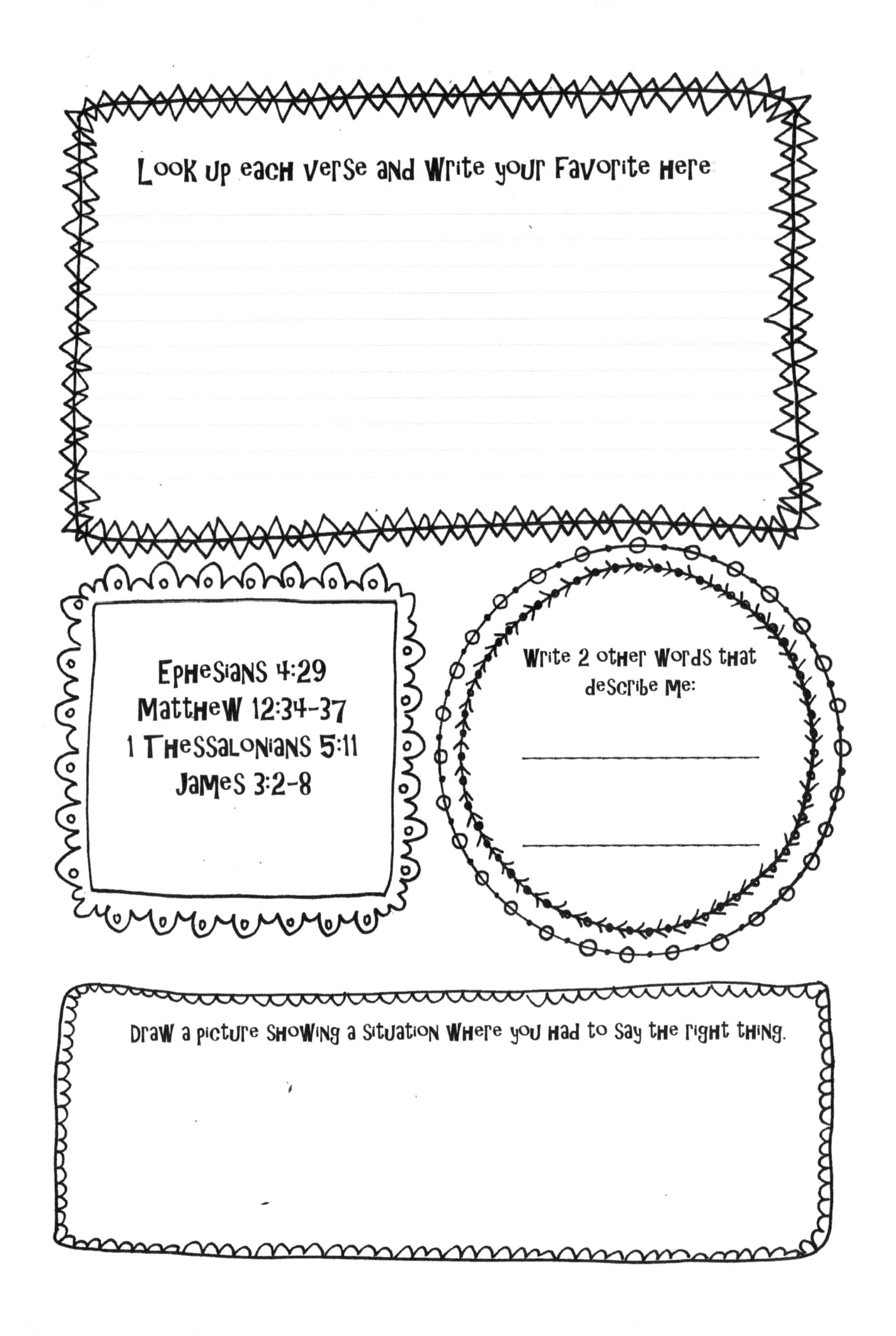

Ephesians 4:29
Matthew 12:34-37
1 Thessalonians 5:11
James 3:2-8

Write 2 other words that describe me:

_____

_____

Draw a picture showing a situation where you had to say the right thing.

SPECH

1 John 3:18

Dear children, let us not love with words or speech but with actions and in truth.

Look up each verse and write your favorite here

Proverbs 11:13
Proverbs 26:20-22
Titus 3:1-2
James 4:11

Write 2 other words that describe me:

_____
_____

Draw a picture showing a situation when someone was hurt by gossip.

GOSSIP

1 Peter 3:9-10

Do not repay evil with evil or insult with insult. On the contrary, repay evil with blessing, because to this you were called so that you may inherit a blessing. For, "Whoever would love life and see good days must keep their tongue from evil and their lips from deceitful speech.

Look up each verse and write your favorite here:

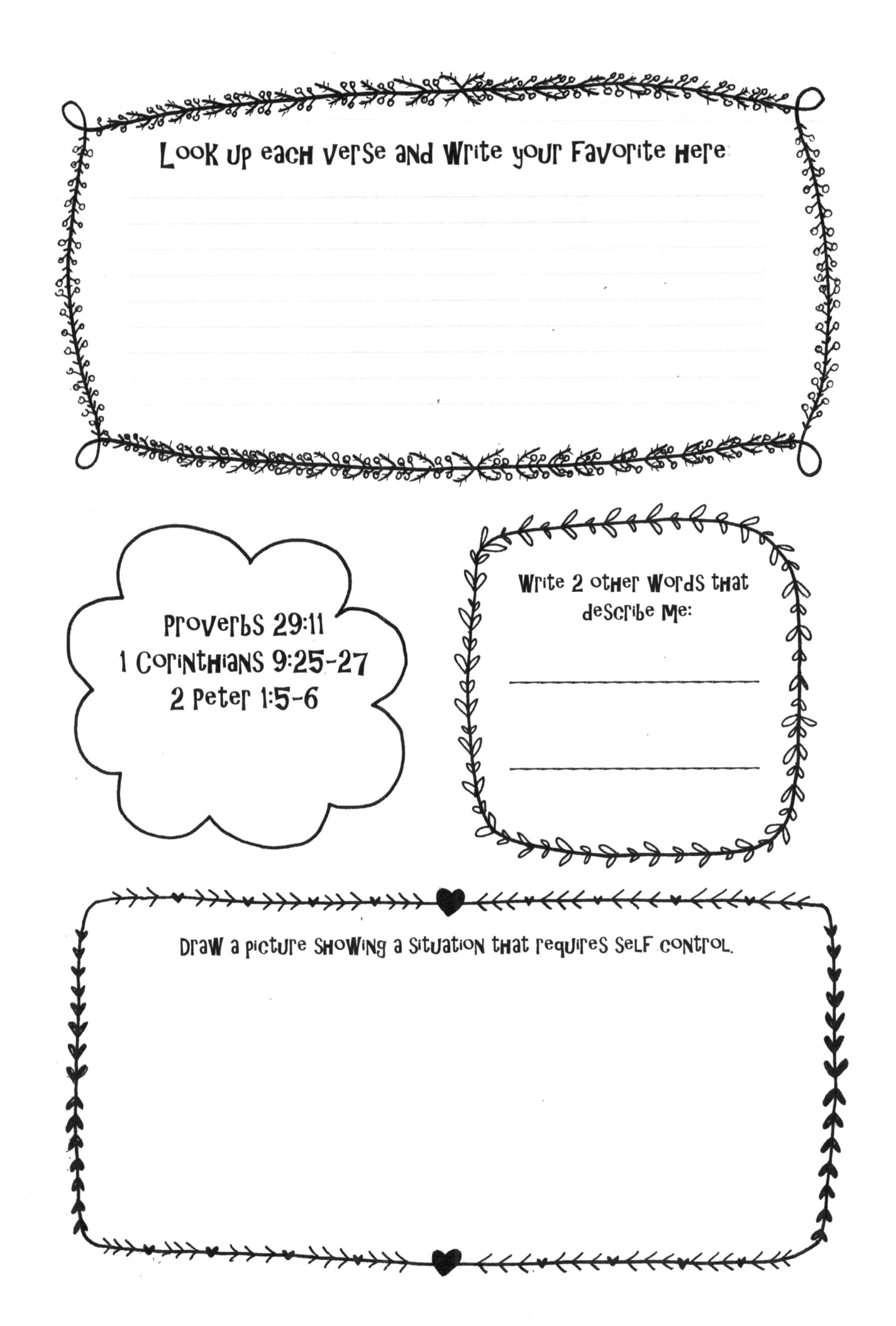

Proverbs 29:11
1 Corinthians 9:25-27
2 Peter 1:5-6

Write 2 other words that describe me:

Draw a picture showing a situation that requires self control.

SELF CONTROL

Proverbs 25:28

Like a city that is broken into and without walls is a man who has no control over his spirit.

Look up each verse and write your favorite here:

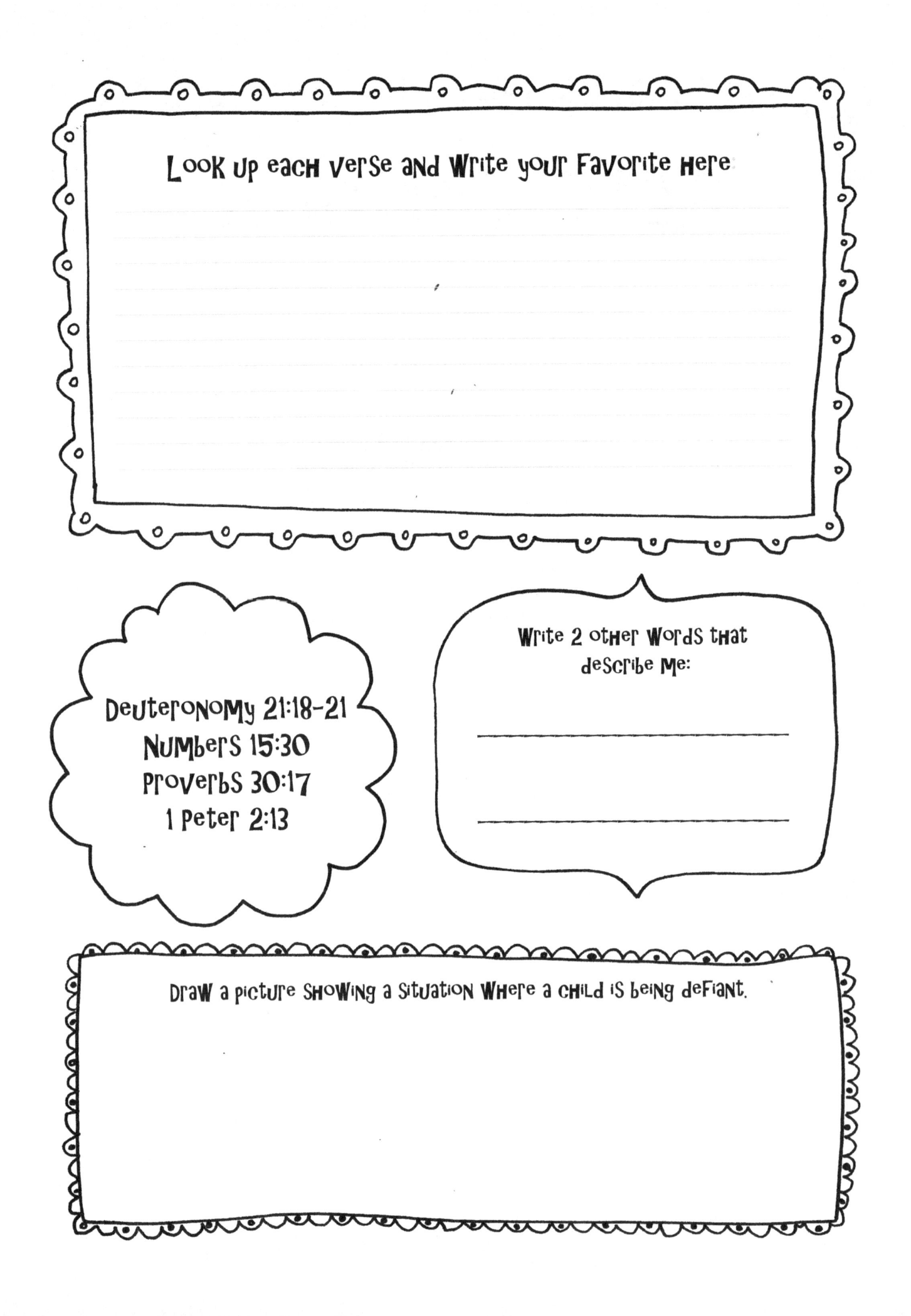

Deuteronomy 21:18-21
Numbers 15:30
Proverbs 30:17
1 Peter 2:13

Write 2 other words that describe me:

_____

_____

Draw a picture showing a situation where a child is being defiant.

DEFIANCE

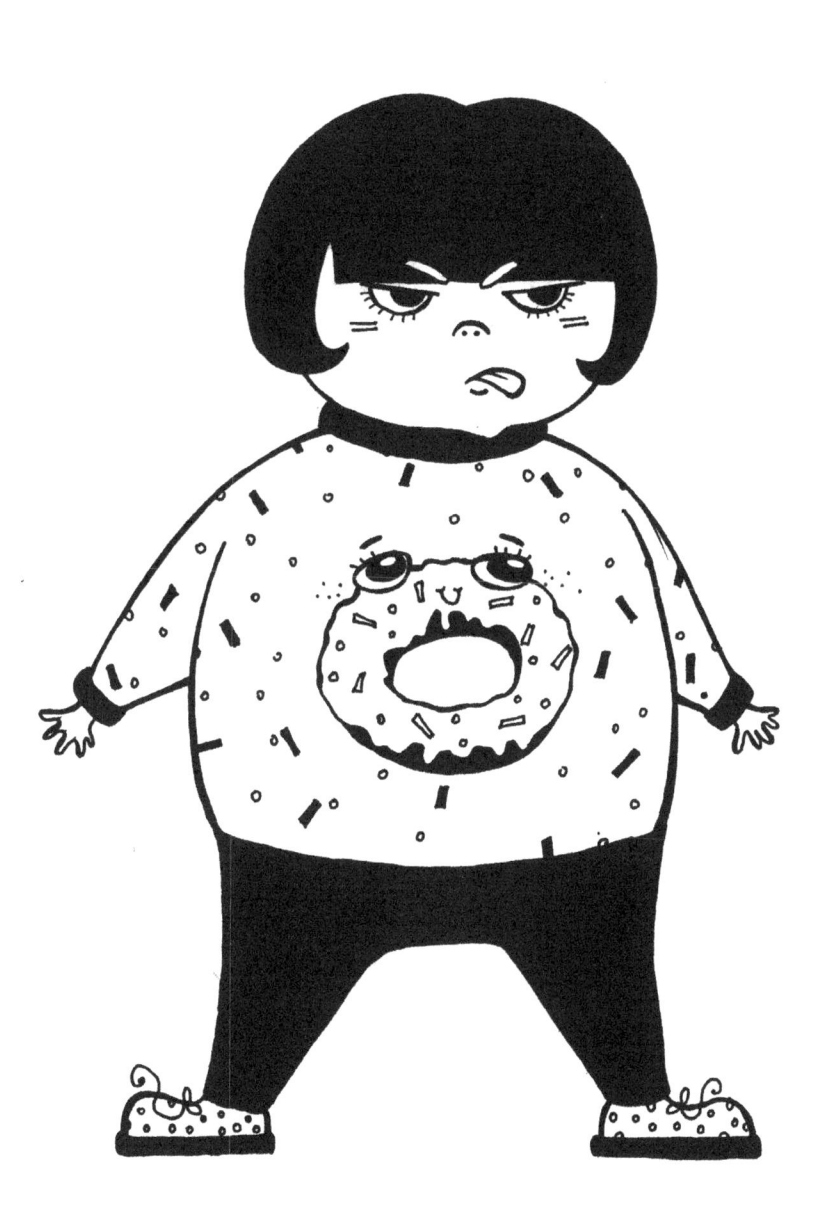

Romans 13:2

Therefore whoever resists authority has opposed the ordinance of God; and they who have opposed will receive condemnation upon themselves.

Look up each verse and write your favorite here:

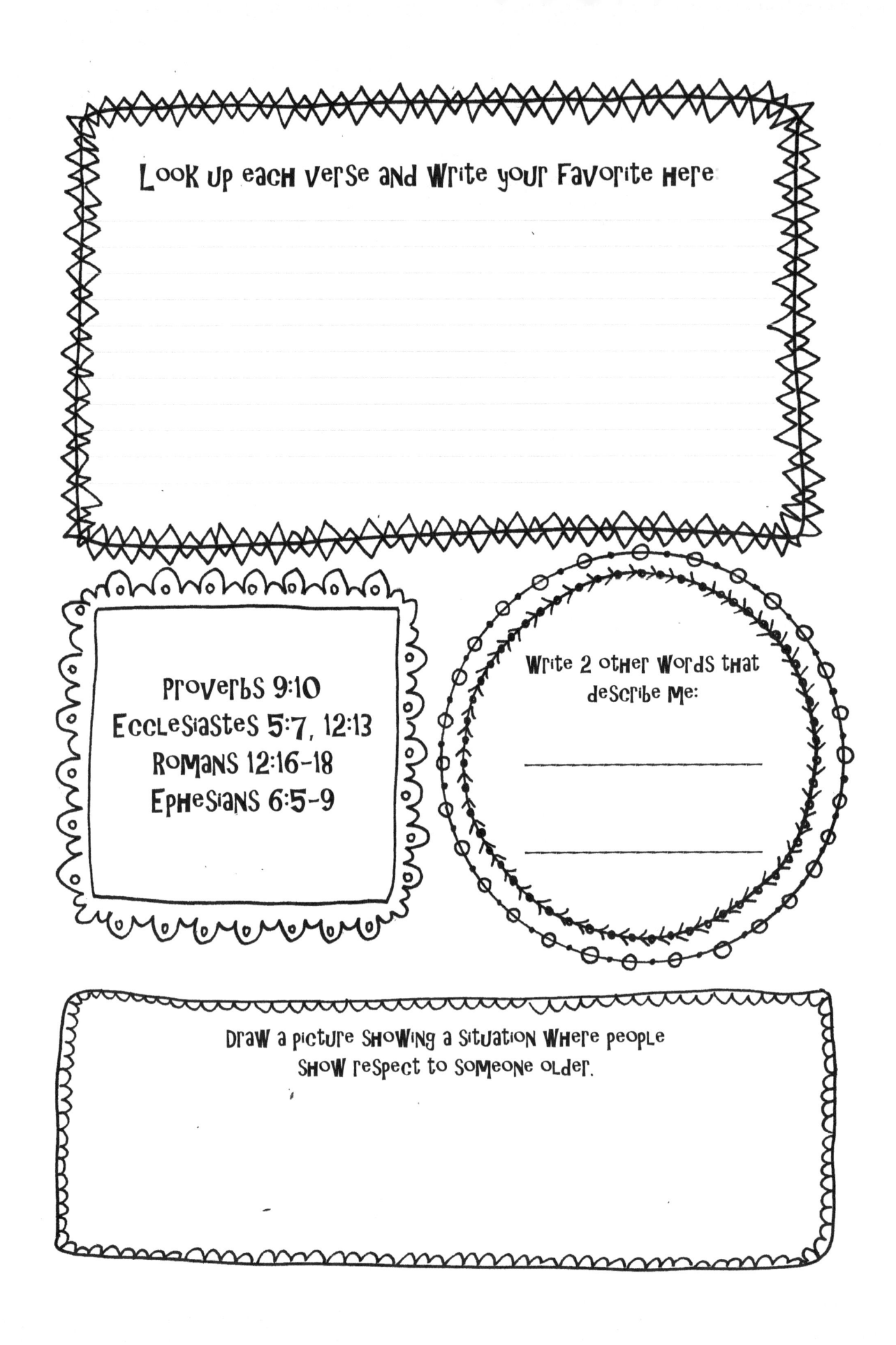

Proverbs 9:10
Ecclesiastes 5:7, 12:13
Romans 12:16-18
Ephesians 6:5-9

Write 2 other words that describe me:

_____
_____

Draw a picture showing a situation where people show respect to someone older.

RESPECT

Ephesians 6:2-3

Honor your father and mother (which is the first commandment with a promise) that it may be well with you, and that you may live long on the earth.

Look up each verse and write your favorite here

Exodus 20:12
Proverbs 13:13
Proverbs 30:17
Ephesians 6:1-2

Write 2 other words that describe me:

_____

_____

Draw a picture showing a situation where a child is disobeying her parents.

DISOBEDIENCE

Colossians 3:20

Children, be obedient to your parents in all things, for this is well pleasing to the Lord.

Look up each verse and write your favorite here:

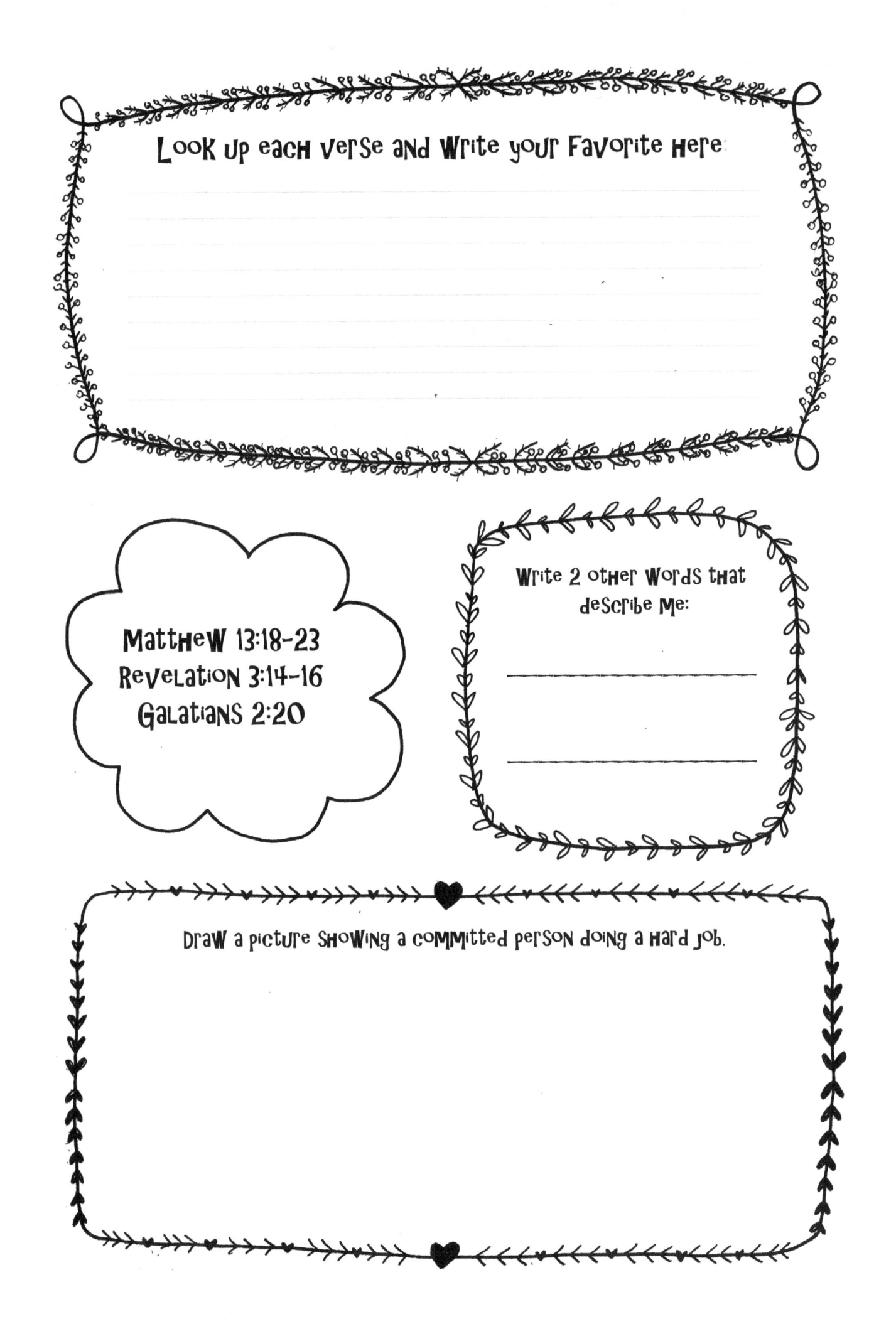

Matthew 13:18-23
Revelation 3:14-16
Galatians 2:20

Write 2 other words that describe me:

Draw a picture showing a committed person doing a hard job.

COMMITMENT

Proverbs **16:3**

Commit your work to the Lord, and your plans will be established.

Look up each verse and Write your Favorite Here

2 Corinthians 8:7
Hebrews 4:16
Acts 20:32
Hebrews 12:15

Write 2 other Words that describe Me:

_____

_____

Draw a picture showing one person being gracious to another.

GRACIOUSNESS

Philippians 4:5

Let your graciousness be known to everyone.

The Lord is near.

Look up each verse and write your favorite here:

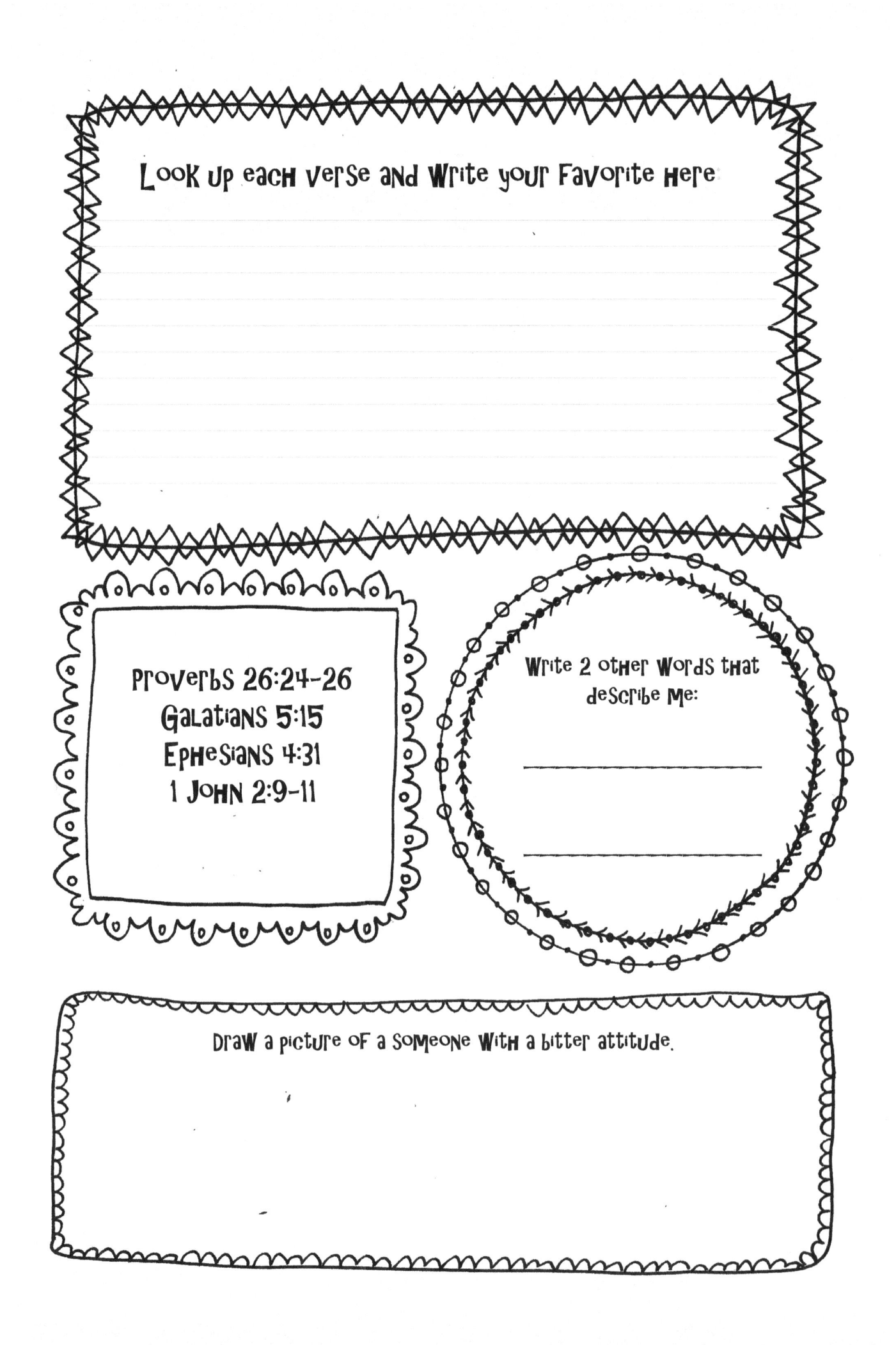

Proverbs 26:24-26
Galatians 5:15
Ephesians 4:31
1 John 2:9-11

Write 2 other words that describe me:

_____

_____

Draw a picture of a someone with a bitter attitude.

BITTERNESS

Hebrews 12:14-15

Pursue peace with all men, and the sanctification without which no one will see the Lord. See to it that no one comes short of the Grace of God: that no root of bitterness springing up causes trouble, and by it many be defiled.

Look up each verse and write your favorite here

Romans 15:13
John 16:22
1 Peter 1:8-9

Write 2 other words that describe me:

_____

_____

Draw a picture showing a situation that made you feel joyful.

JOY

Zephaniah 3:17

The Lord your God is with you, the Mighty Warrior who saves. He will take great delight in you; in his love he will no longer rebuke you, but will rejoice over you with singing.

Look up each verse and write your favorite here

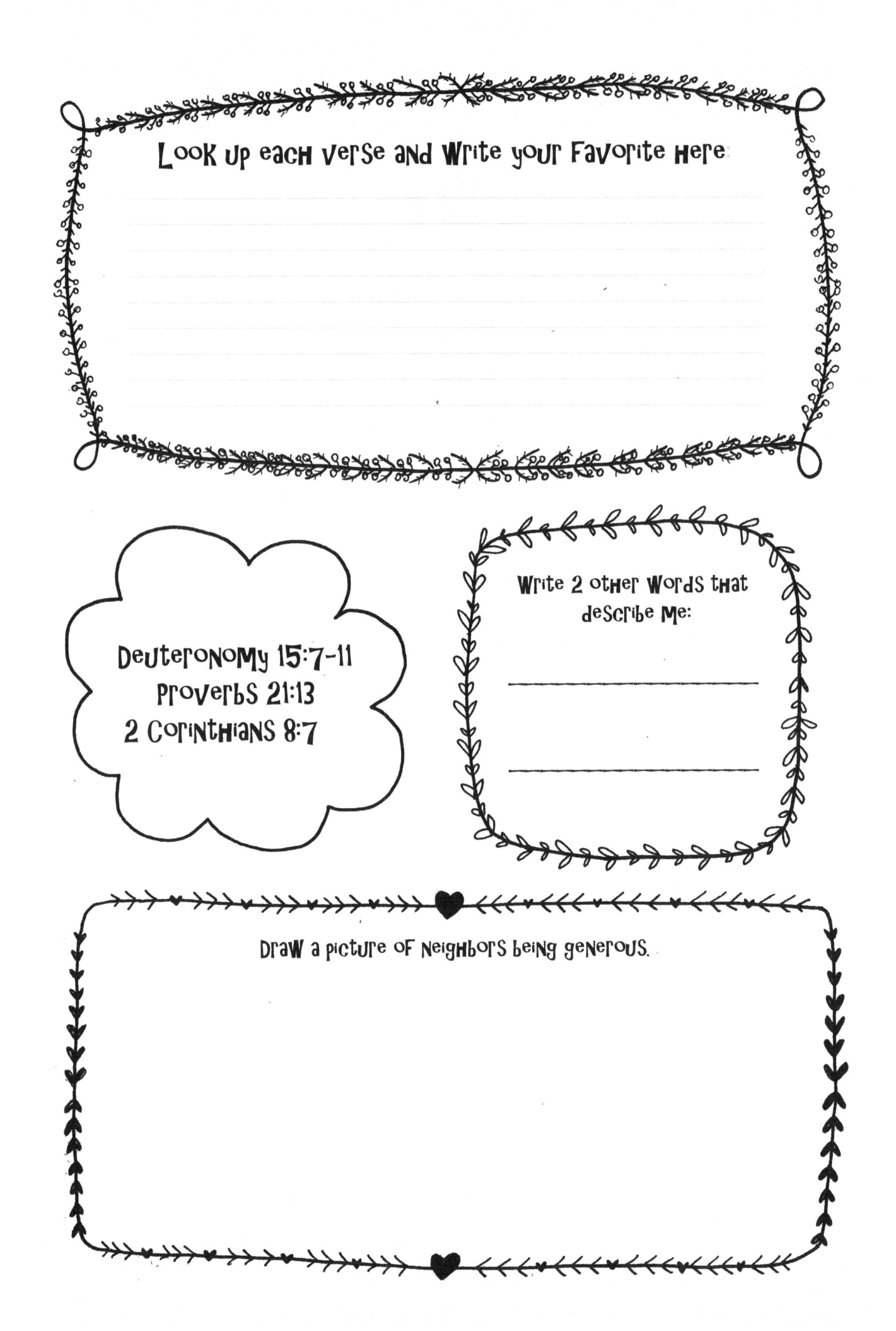

Deuteronomy 15:7-11
Proverbs 21:13
2 Corinthians 8:7

Write 2 other words that describe me:

_____

_____

Draw a picture of neighbors being generous.

GENEROSITY

1 John 3:17

But whoever has the world's goods, and beholds his brother in need and closes his heart against him, how does the love of God abide in him?

Look up each verse and write your favorite here:

Proverbs 23:17
Romans 13:13
Galatians 5:26
1 Peter 2:1-2

Write 2 other words that describe me:

_____

_____

Draw a picture showing a situation that made you feel ENVIOUS.

ENVY

1 Corinthians 13:4

Love...is not jealous

Look up each verse and write your favorite here

Luke 6:35
1 Corinthians 13:4
Ephesians 4:29
Colossians 3:12

Write 2 other words that describe me:

_____

_____

Draw a picture showing a situation of a time someone was kind to you.

KINDNESS

Colossians 4:6

Let your speech always be with grace, as though seasoned with salt, so that you will know how to respond to each person.

Look up each verse and write your favorite here

Proverbs 13:1,18
Proverbs 13:10
James 1:19-20
1 Corinthians 1:11-13
Philippians 2:1-11
1 Timothy 3:3

Write 2 other words that describe me:

_____
_____

Draw a picture showing siblings forgiving each other after a quarrel.

QUARRELING

Colossians 3:8

But now you must also rid yourselves of all such things as these: anger, rage, malice, slander, and filthy language from your lips.

Look up each verse and write your favorite here

Luke 6:35
Romans 12:9
John 13:35

Write 2 other words that describe me:

_____

_____

Draw a picture of your family on your birthday.

LOVE

1 Peter 4:8

Above all, love each other deeply, because love covers over a multitude of sins.

Look up each verse and write your favorite here

Proverbs 1:7
1 Corinthians 1:25
James 3:17

Write 2 other words that describe me:

_____

_____

Draw a picture of three wise people you know.

WISDOM

James 3:17

But the wisdom that comes from heaven is first of all pure; then peace-loving, considerate, submissive, full of mercy and good fruit, impartial and sincere.

Look up each verse and write your favorite here:

Proverbs 8:13
Galatians 6:3-4
James 4:6
2 Timothy 2:24-26

Write 2 other words that describe me:

_____

_____

Draw a picture of a person who thinks they are better than everyone else.

PRIDE

look at me

1 Peter 5:5-6

In the same way, you who are younger, submit yourselves to your elders. All of you, clothe yourselves with humility toward one another, because, "God opposes the proud but shows favor to the humble." Humble yourselves, therefore, under God's mighty hand, that he may lift you up in due time.

Look up each verse and write your favorite here

Psalm 37:11, 138:6, 149:4
Proverbs 29:23
Zephaniah 3:11-12
Mark 9:33-35

Write 2 other words that describe me:
_____
_____

Draw a picture showing a situation that made you feel humble.

HUMILITY

Ephesians 4:2

Be completely humble and gentle; be patient, bearing with one another in love.

Look up each verse and write your favorite here:

Mark 10:42-45
1 John 3:16
Mark 10:28-31

Write 2 other words that describe Me:

Draw a picture showing a situation that required a big sacrifice.

SELF-SACRIFICE

Luke 9:23-24

And He was saying to them all, "If anyone wishes to come after me, let him deny himself, and take up his cross daily and follow me. For whoever wishes to save his life will lose it, but whoever loses his life for My sake, he is the one who will save it.

Look up each verse and write your favorite here

Matthew 18:21-22
Luke 17:3-4
Mark 11:25-26

Write 2 other words that describe me:

_____

_____

Draw a picture showing how you feel after someone forgives you.

FORGIVENESS

Colossians 3:13

Bear with each other and forgive one another if any of you has a grievance against someone. Forgive as the Lord forgave you.

Look up each verse and write your favorite here:

Matthew 7:3-5
1 Timothy 4:2
1 Peter 2:1
James 4:8

Write 2 other words that describe me:
_____
_____

Draw a picture showing a person who says one thing, but does another.

HYPOCRISY

1 John 1:6

If we say we have fellowship with Him and yet walk in darkness, we lie and do not practice the truth

Look up each verse and write your favorite here

Philippians 4:8
3 John 1:4
John 8:32

Write 2 other words that describe me:
_____
_____

Draw a picture showing a situation when you told the truth.

TRUTH

1 John 1:6

If we claim to have fellowship with him and yet walk in the darkness, we lie and do not live out the truth.

Look up each verse and write your favorite here:

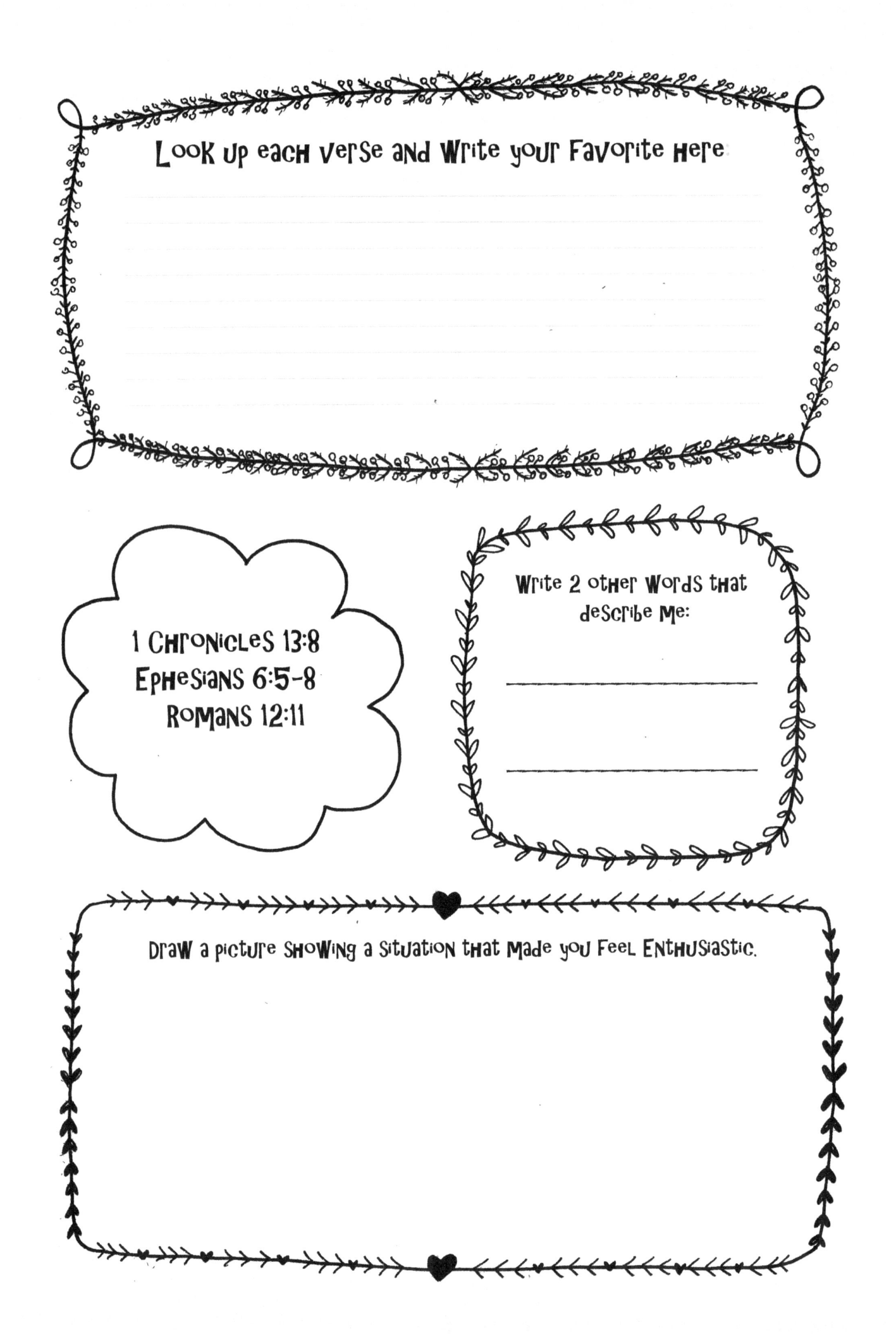

1 Chronicles 13:8
Ephesians 6:5-8
Romans 12:11

Write 2 other words that describe me:

_____

_____

Draw a picture showing a situation that made you feel enthusiastic.

ENTHUSIASM

Colossians 3:23

Whatever you do, do your work heartily, as for the Lord rather than for men

Look up each verse and write your favorite here:

Proverbs 12:24
Proverbs 6:6-11
Proverbs 20:13
2 Thessalonians 3:10

Write 2 other words that describe me:

_____

_____

Draw a picture of what you were doing last time you were being SLOTHFUL.

SLOTHFULNESS

1 Corinthians 10:31

Whether, then. you eat or drink or whatever you do ,
do all to the glory of God.

Look up each verse and write your favorite here:

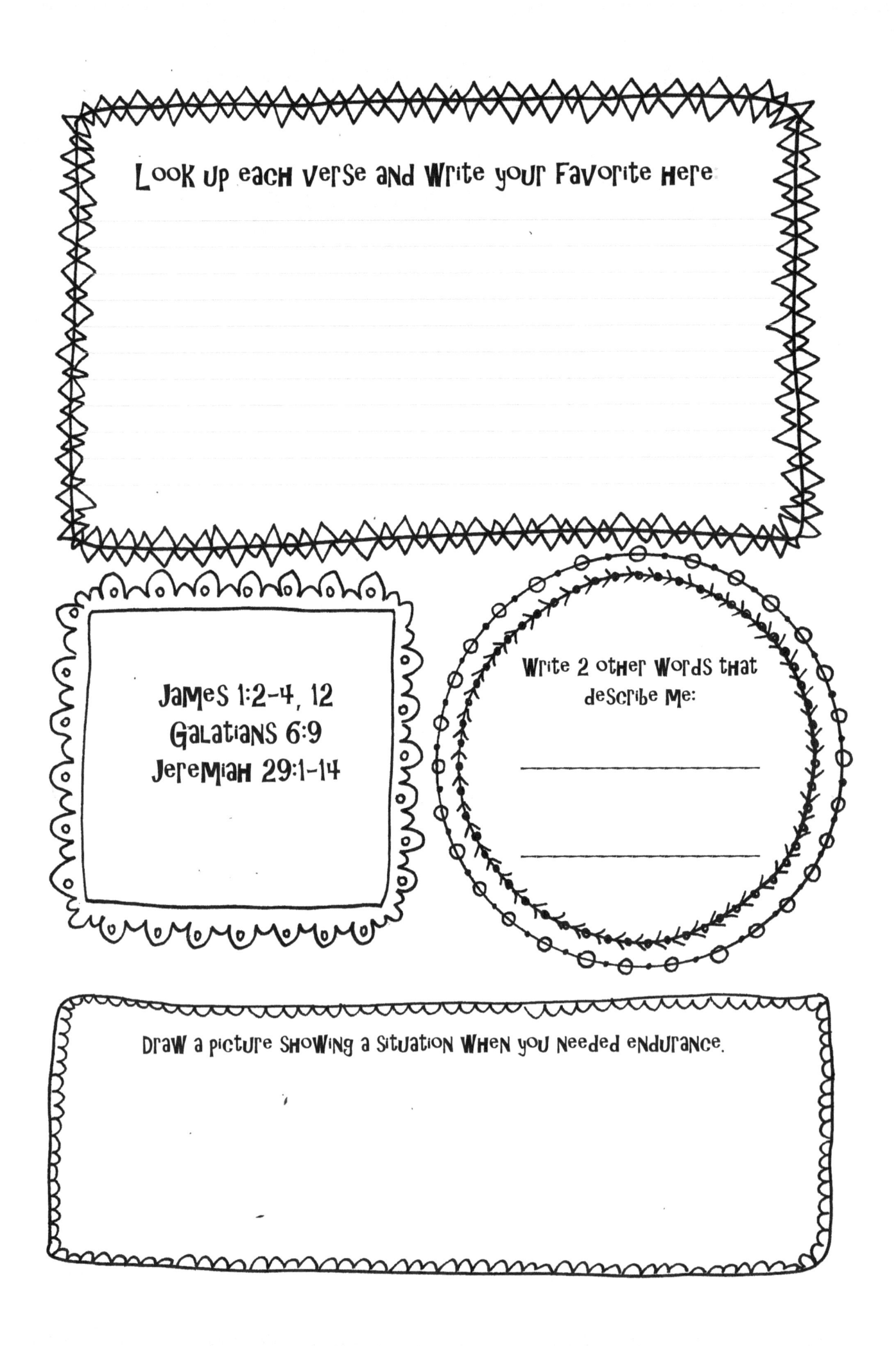

James 1:2-4, 12
Galatians 6:9
Jeremiah 29:1-14

Write 2 other words that describe me:

_____

_____

Draw a picture showing a situation when you needed endurance.

ENDURANCE

Romans 5:3-4

Not only so, but we also glory in our sufferings, because we know that suffering produces perseverance;

perseverance, character; and character, hope.

Look up each verse and write your favorite here:

Proverbs 24:11-12
Matthew 25:14-30
Nehemiah 10:32, 35

Write 2 other words that describe me:
_____
_____

Draw a picture of you being reasonable to finish your chores well..

RESPONSIBILITY

Galatians 6:4-5

But let each one test his own work, and then his reason to boast will be in himself alone and not in his neighbor. For each will have to bear his own load.

Look up each verse and write your favorite here

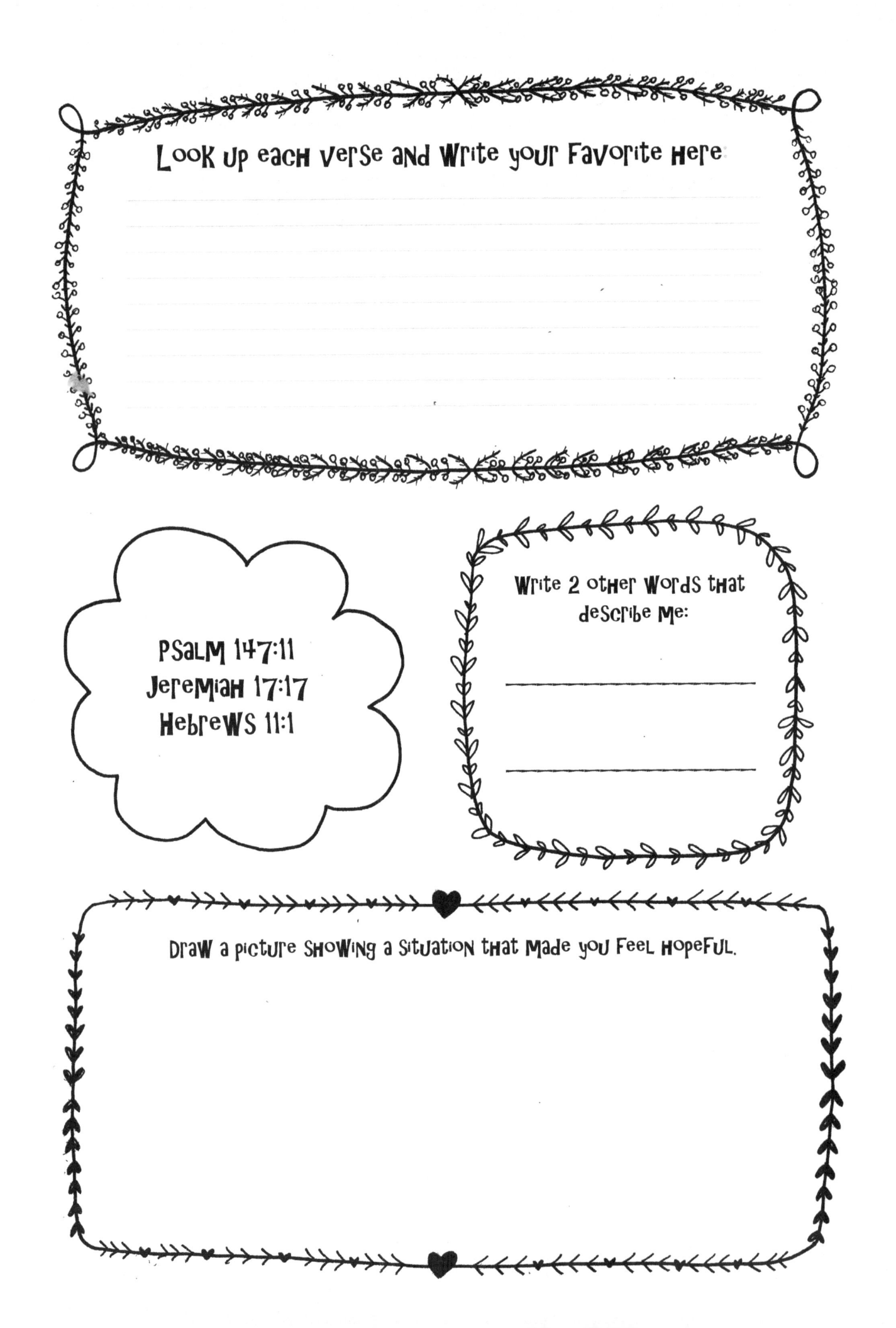

Psalm 147:11
Jeremiah 17:17
Hebrews 11:1

Write 2 other words that describe me:

_____

_____

Draw a picture showing a situation that made you feel hopeful.

HOPE

Romans 5:2-5

Through whom also we have access by faith into this grace in which we stand, and rejoice in hope of the glory of God. And not only that, but we also glory in tribulations, knowing that tribulation produces perseverance; and perseverance, character; and character, hope. Now hope does not disappoint, because the love of God has been poured out in our hearts by the Holy Spirit who was given to us.

Look up each verse and write your favorite here

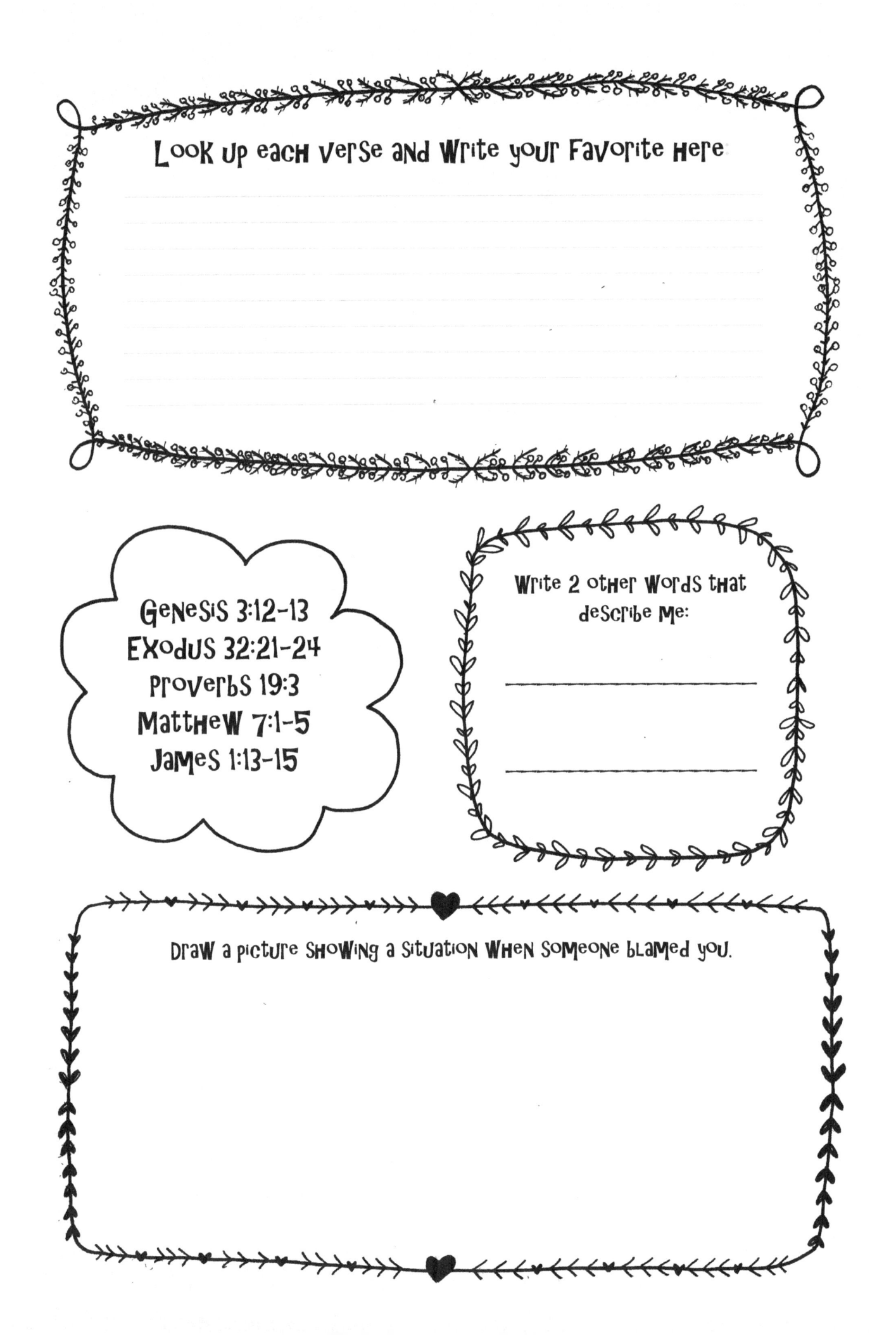

Genesis 3:12-13
Exodus 32:21-24
Proverbs 19:3
Matthew 7:1-5
James 1:13-15

Write 2 other words that describe me:
_____
_____

Draw a picture showing a situation when someone blamed you.

BLAME SHIFTING

Proverbs 28:13

He who conceals his transgressions will not prosper, but he who confesses and forsakes them will find compassion.

Look up each verse and write your favorite here

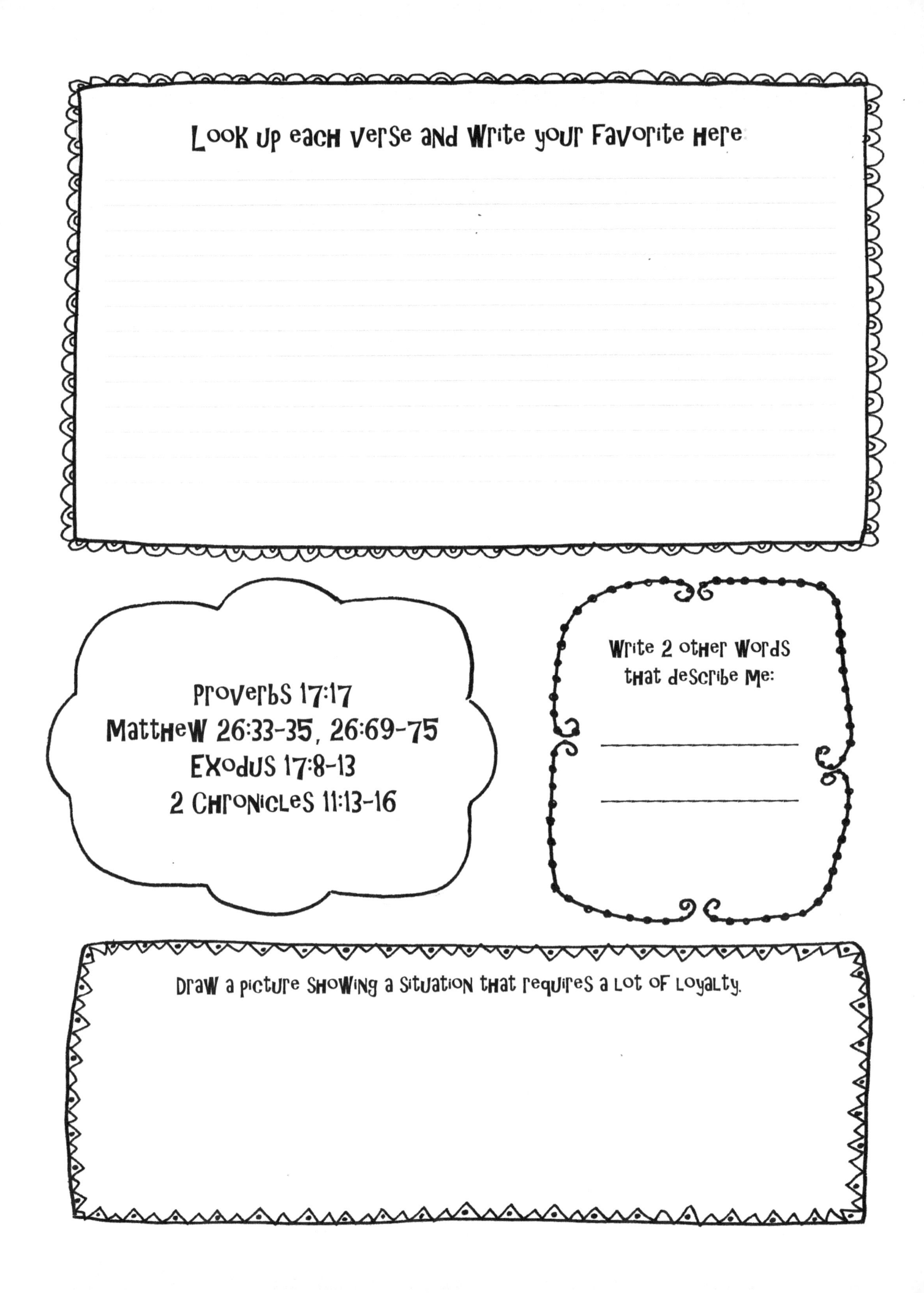

Proverbs 17:17
Matthew 26:33-35, 26:69-75
Exodus 17:8-13
2 Chronicles 11:13-16

Write 2 other words that describe me:

_____

_____

Draw a picture showing a situation that requires a lot of loyalty.

LOYALTY

Hebrews 10:23

Let us hold fast the confession of our hope without wavering, for He who promised is faithful;

Look up each verse and write your favorite here

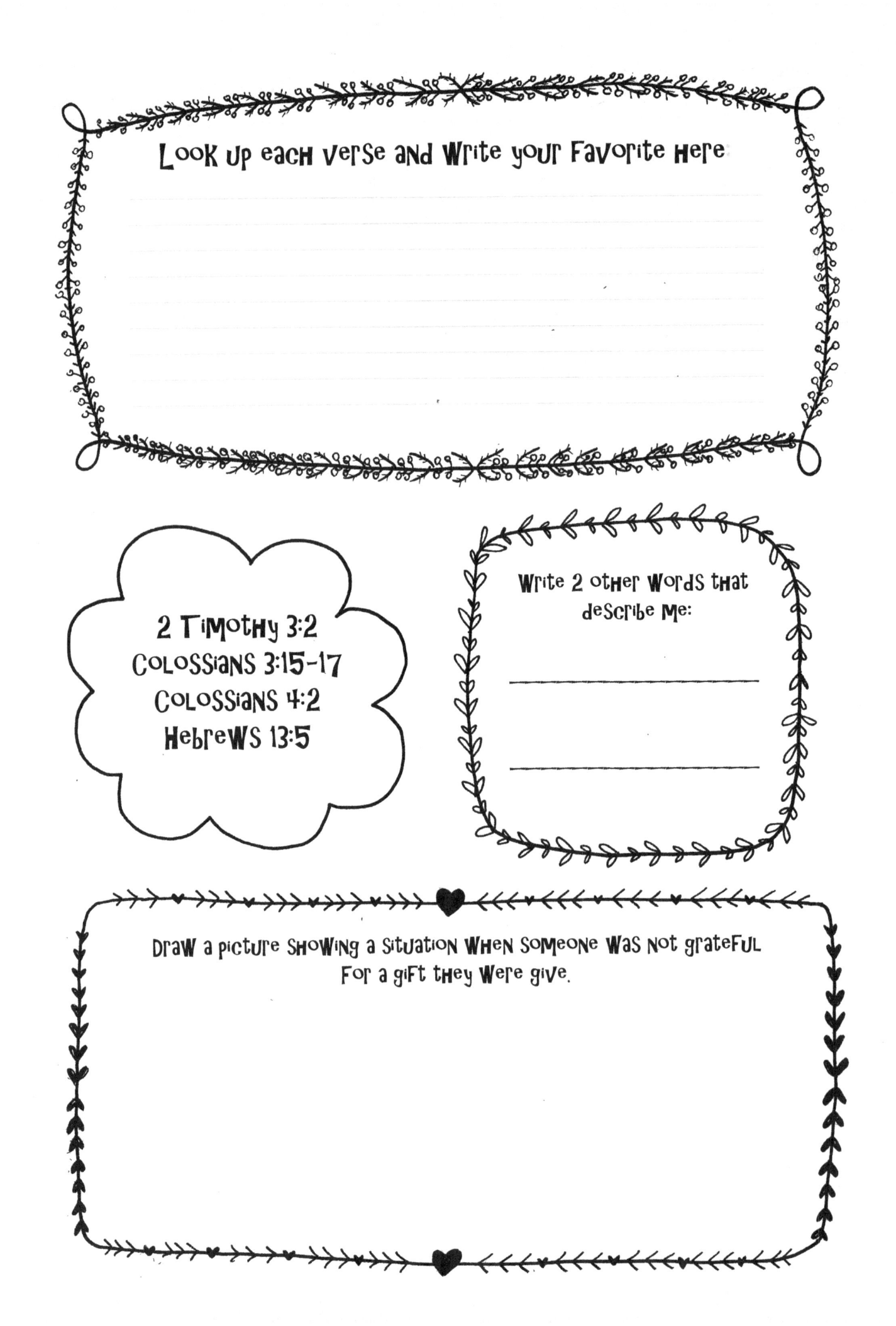

2 Timothy 3:2
Colossians 3:15-17
Colossians 4:2
Hebrews 13:5

Write 2 other words that describe me:

_____

_____

Draw a picture showing a situation when someone was not grateful for a gift they were give.

UNGRATEFULNESS

1 Thessalonians 5:18

In everything give thanks; for this is God's will for you in Christ Jesus.

Look up each verse and write your favorite here

1 Corinthians 6:19-20
James 1:27
Romans 12:10
Proverbs 21:21

Write 2 other words that describe me:

_____

_____

Draw a picture showing how you honor God.

HONOR

John 12:24-26

Very truly I tell you, unless a kernel of wheat falls to the ground and dies, it remains only a single seed. But if it dies, it produces many seeds. Anyone who loves their life will lose it, while anyone who hates their life in this world will keep it for eternal life. Whoever serves me must follow me; and where I am, my servant also will be. My Father will honor the one who serves me.

Look up each verse and write your favorite here

Psalm 37:7-9
Lamentations 3:26-27
Galatians 6:9
James 1:19
2 Timothy 2:24

Write 2 other words that describe me:

_____

_____

Draw a picture showing a situation that required you to be patient.

PATIENCE

Romans **12:12**

Be joyful in hope, patient in affliction, faithful in prayer.

Look up each verse and write your favorite here

Psalm 15:4-5
Proverbs 6:1-5
Matthew 21:28-32
Colossians 3:9

Write 2 other words that describe me:
_____
_____

Draw a picture showing two old people who love each other for life.

FAITHFULNESS

Matthew 5:37

Simply let your "yes" be "yes", and your "no",
"no" anything beyond this comes from the evil one

Look up each verse and write your favorite here

1 Peter 3:11
James 3:18
Psalm 29:11
Romans 12:18

Write 2 other words that describe me:

_____

_____

Draw a picture of a peaceful place.

PEACE

Hebrews **12:14**

Make every effort to live in peace with everyone and to be holy; without holiness no one will see the Lord.

Look up each verse and write your favorite here:

1 Corinthians 11:34
1 Corinthians 15:23

Write 2 other words that describe me:

_____

_____

Draw a picture showing what your room looks like after your friends visit.

DISORDERLINESS

1 Corinthians 14:40

Let all things be done decently and in order.

Look up each verse and write your favorite here:

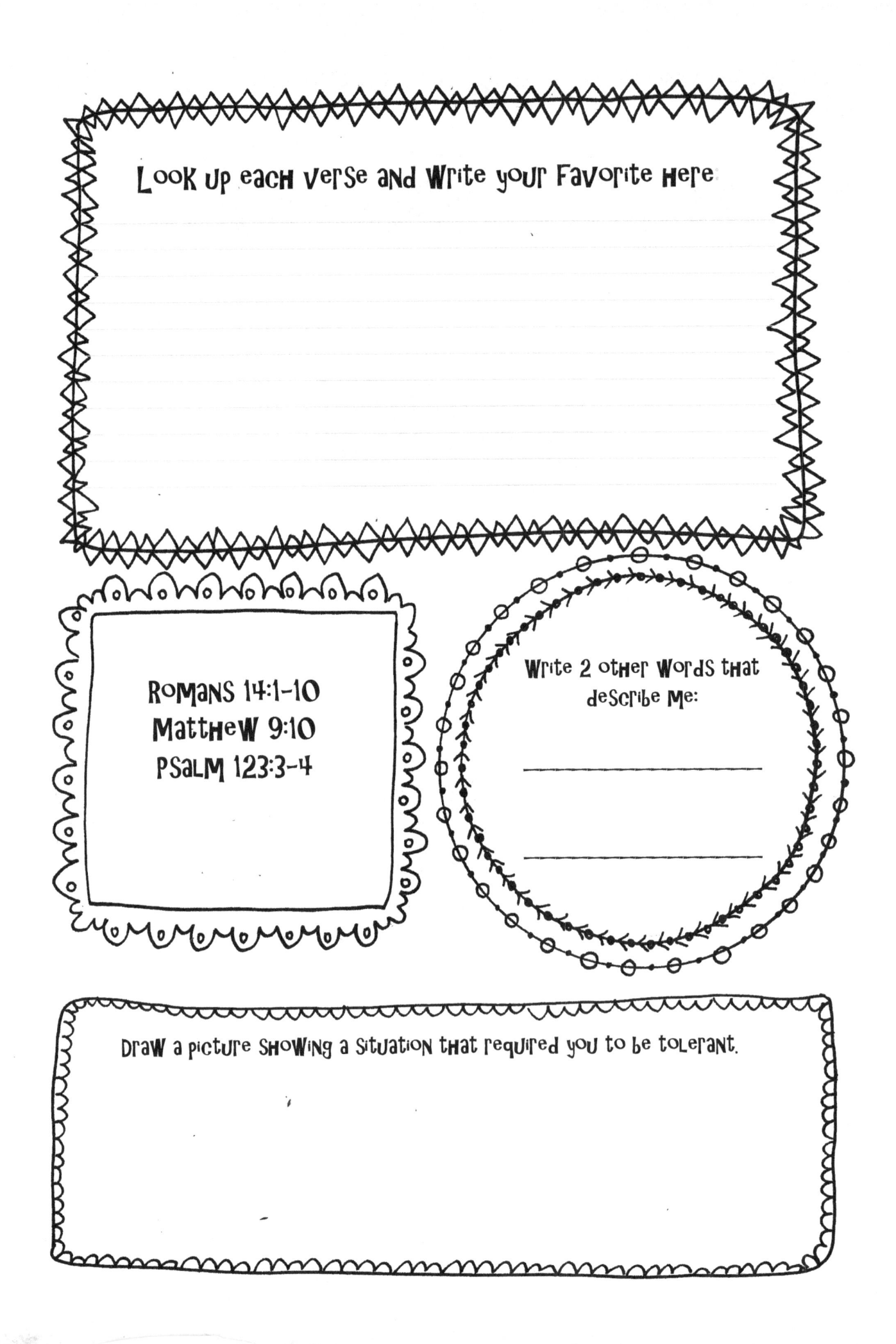

Romans 14:1-10
Matthew 9:10
Psalm 123:3-4

Write 2 other words that describe me:

_____

_____

Draw a picture showing a situation that required you to be tolerant.

TOLERANCE

2 Timothy 4:1-2

I charge you in the presence of God and of Christ Jesus, who is to judge the living and the dead, and by his appearing and his kingdom: preach the word; be ready in season and out of season; reprove, rebuke, and exhort, with complete patience and teaching.

Look up each verse and write your favorite here

Leviticus 19:35-36
Psalm 25:21
Proverbs 28:6
Zechariah 8:16-17

Write 2 other words that describe me:

_____

_____

Draw a picture showing a person showing integrity.

INTEGRITY

Proverbs **11:3**

The integrity of the upright guides them,

but the unfaithful are destroyed by their duplicity.

Look up each verse and write your favorite here

Romans 2:7-8
Romans 5:3-4
2 Corinthians 4:16

Write 2 other words that describe me:

_____

_____

Draw a picture showing a situation that required you persevere.

PERSEVERANCE

Colossians 1:11-12

being strengthened with all power according to his glorious might so that you may have great endurance and patience, and giving joyful thanks to the Father, who has qualified you to share in the inheritance of his holy people in the kingdom of light.

Look up each verse and write your favorite here:

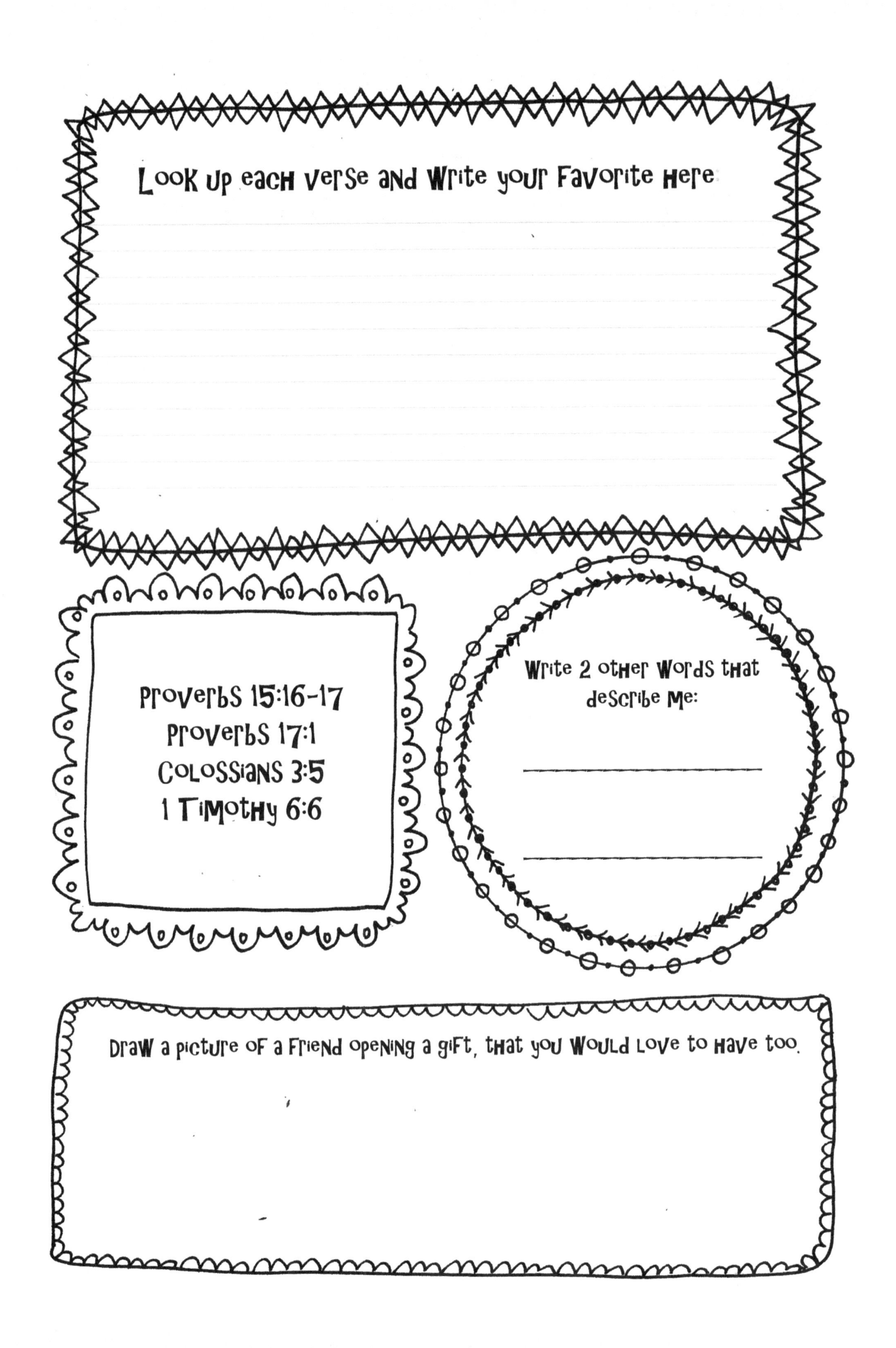

Proverbs 15:16-17
Proverbs 17:1
Colossians 3:5
1 Timothy 6:6

Write 2 other words that describe me:

_____

_____

Draw a picture of a friend opening a gift, that you would love to have too.

COVETING

Luke **12:15**

And He said to them, "Take heed and beware of covetousness, for one's life does not consist in the abundance of things he possesses.

Look up each verse and write your favorite here

1 Chronicles 9:22
1 Corinthians 4:2-4
Ephesians 6:5-8

Write 2 other words that describe me:

_____
_____

Draw a picture showing a situation that required you to be reliable.

RELIABILITY

Luke 16:10

One who is faithful in a very little is also faithful in much, and one who is dishonest in a very little is also dishonest in much.

Look up each verse and write your favorite here:

Matthew 19:16-30
Habakkuk 1:5
2 Kings 6:16-17

Write 2 other words that describe me:

_____

_____

Draw a picture of what you dream of doing for God in the future.

VISION

Proverbs 29:18

Where there is no vision, the people are unrestrained, But happy is he who keeps the law.

Look up each verse and write your favorite here

Matthew 19:16-30
Habakkuk 1:5
2 Kings 6:16-17

Write 2 other words that describe me:

_____

_____

Draw a picture of the kids your parents don't let you hang out with.

BAD COMPANY

1 Corinthians 15:33

Do not be deceived: Bad Company corrupts good morals.

Look up each verse and write your favorite here

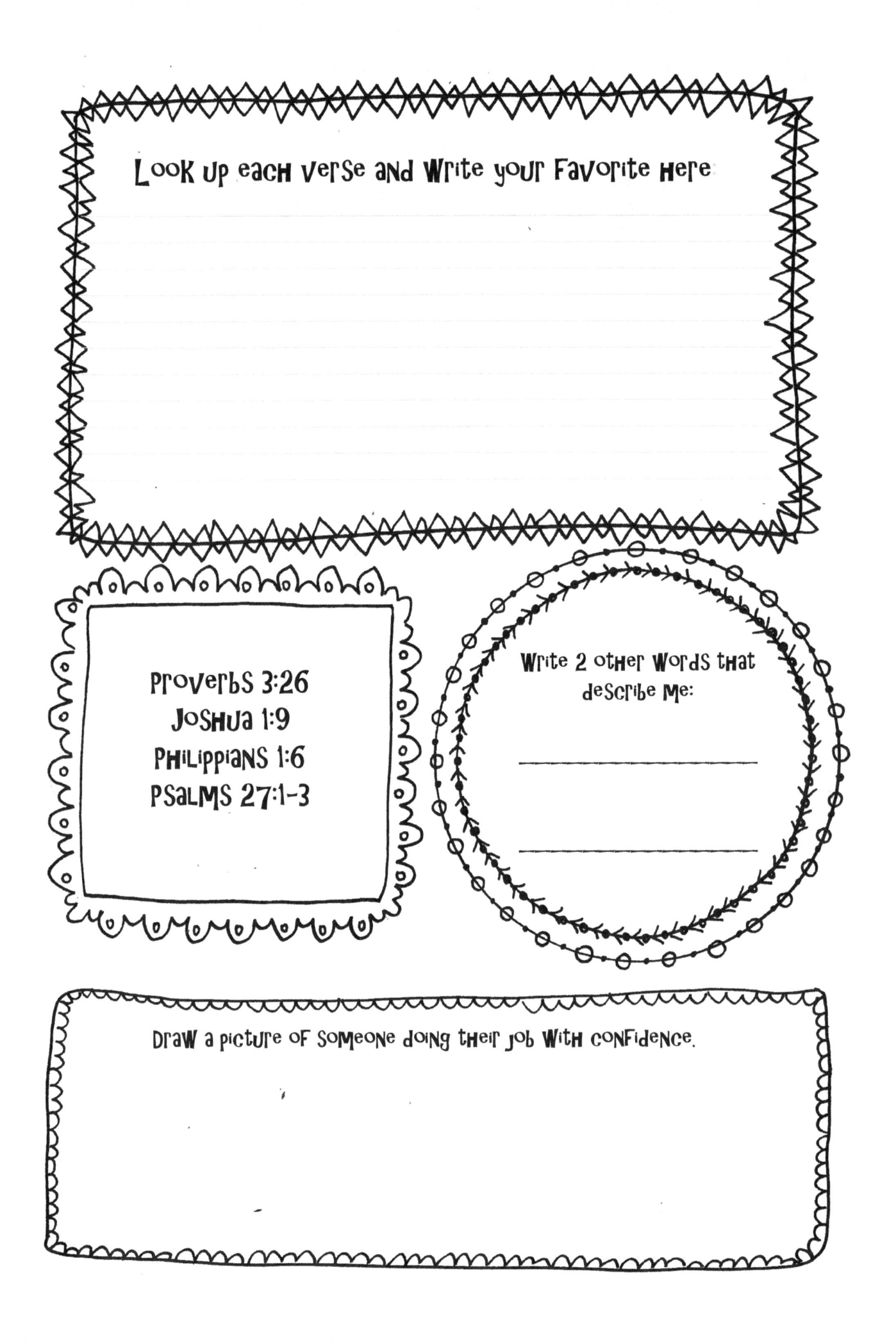

Proverbs 3:26
Joshua 1:9
Philippians 1:6
Psalms 27:1-3

Write 2 other words that describe me:

_____

_____

Draw a picture of someone doing their job with confidence.

CONFIDENCE

Philippians 4:13

I can do all things through Christ which strengthens me.

The Thinking Tree
FUN-SCHOOLING JOURNALS

Copyright Information

You may make copies of these materials for only the children in your household. All other uses of this material must be permitted in writing by the Thinking Tree LLC. It is a violation of copyright law to distribute the electronic files or make copies for your friends, associates or students without our permission.

Contact Us:

The Thinking Tree LLC
317.622.8852 PHONE (Dial +1 outside of the USA)
267.712.7889 FAX

FunSchoolingBooks.com

Made in the USA
Columbia, SC
06 April 2019